Passive Income

How to Make Money Online Through Affiliate Marketing

Peter Becker

Copyright © 2016 by Peter Becker

All rights reserved. This book or any portion thereof may not be reproduced or used in any manner whatsoever without the express written permission of the publisher except for the use of brief quotations in a book review.

Table of Content

INTRODUCTION

THE BASICS OF AFFILIATE MARKETING
Finding The Right Affiliate Programs
The Best Of The Bunch
e-Product Networks
Secondary Affiliate Programs

PROS & CONS OF AFFILIATE MARKETING
Promoting Low-Quality Products May Negatively Affect Your Reputation
Low Product Commission Can Harm Your Affiliate Marketing Business
Affiliate Marketing Can Become Isolating Shutdown Of The Affiliate Company Or The Products Hijacked Affiliate Links
Close To Nothing Start-Up Costs
Learn While You Work
Creating A Global Market For Your Affiliate Products
Do What You Love By Choosing A Niche You Love Earn Passive Income with affiliate marketing

Avoid The Hassle Of Physically Handing The Products

CHOOSING THE BEST NICHE FOR YOURSELF
How To Brainstorm Brilliant Ideas For Your Potential Niche
What Are Your Hobbies?
What Are You Friends' Hobbies?
Research The Internet
Pay attention to the supply side of the equation
Accessories
Everywhere Browse Through Magazines
Limit Your Niche While Still Leaving Room For Expansion
Ensure An Audience Is There And That You'll Be Able To Reach Them
Ensure You're Willing To Do What It Takes
Verify That There Are Multiple Revenue Streams Within The Niche
Check Out Whether Or Not The Niche Is Defensible

AFFILIATE MARKETING THROUGH BLOGGING
Build An Email Listing
Build A Relationship With Your Subscribers

AFFILIATE MARKETING THROUGH PODCASTING

STRATEGIES TO MAKE THE MOST OF AFFILIATE MARKETING

Trying To Achieve Too Much, Too Soon

Create Content That Your Competition Can't Compete With

Build A Brand That Adds Value

Keep The Mobile In Mind Keep Track Of Breakout And Seasonal Trends

Aim For Topic Targeting Instead Of Keyword Targeting

CONCLUSION

Money Making Mindset

RESOURCES & EXAMPLES

"If opportunity doesn't knock, build a door" – Milton Berle

Introduction

Have you ever found yourself wondering why bloggers would create videos or write articles just so people could access them for free? Why do they take out time every day to create a following for themselves? Why are these people, at the end of the day, called **professional** bloggers?

If you've found yourself asking these questions, you're not alone. I'm sure you've found it hard to believe that bloggers actually earn a living. Well, let me tell you a secret. One of the ways they do this, which is probably the best way to earn money online, is through **affiliate marketing**.

You've probably heard this term before but aren't quite sure what it means. Well, affiliate marketing is basically internet advertising that allows online business to affiliate themselves with countless website owners, commonly known as publishers or affiliate, through affiliate programs. Affiliates usually make money by generating traffic, sales, and leads for businesses.

Affiliate marketing is one of the best ways to earn passive income. Passive income is your ticket to a free world. Well, not exactly, but it IS your ticket to a flexible and easy work schedule. Through the passive income approach, you have full authority to decide how many vacations you want to take and achieve the easiest lifestyle you can possibly get.

From the sounds of it, affiliate marketing seems pretty simple, doesn't it? All you need to do is link yourself to some business and just sell their product, right?
Wrong.

Although the entire concept of affiliate marketing is based on the idea of selling a product without investing the time and effort of making, it's more than that. Affiliate marketing isn't just a game of luck and requires several trial and errors to get it right.

However, once you do, there's no better way to earn easy money. In the words of Bo Bennett, *"Affiliate marketing has made businesses millions and ordinary people millionaires."*

So, tell me, do you want to be one of these 'ordinary people'? I know you do and that's what this book is here for! ***"Passive Income: How To Make Money Online Through Affiliate Marketing"*** is not only going to give you an idea of the basics of affiliate marketing, but it'll also give you insights on the affiliate marketing strategies experts usually swear by.

ONE

THE BASICS OF AFFILIATE MARKETING

You've probably found yourself asking how bloggers are completely at ease with their lives and, yet, still manage to earn a hefty income. Now, with this chapter, you'll start to get an idea of how all this is possible. Passive income allows you to attain financial freedom; a goal most of us aim to achieve. What exactly does this goal entail? Well, in simple terms, financial freedom basically refers to a position when your income easily covers your expenses. It lets you attain the ideal position where you can fulfill your wants and needs with minimal time and effort.

How affiliate marketing comes into play is quite simple. Affiliate marketing is a means of earning passive income which, in turn, is a way of attaining financial freedom. Seems pretty straightforward, right?

Now that you've entered the world of affiliate marketing, allow me to explain what it really is. Affiliate marketing gives you the opportunity to recommend a variety of products and services from other companies and earn a commission when someone you've recommended the product to actually buys the product. In order to keep track of how many purchases are being made as a result of your recommendation, the merchant will give you a link unique that you need to use when linking your followers to their website. This link contains a referral code that has specifically been assigned to you. If people click the link you've provided and purchase the product or service within a timeframe given to you by your merchant, you'll earn a commission on the sale. Furthermore, one of the best parts about this is that the products will cost consumers the same amount of money if they purchase it through you, which means that they won't be losing anything by following your recommendation. Hence, instead of charging consumers a higher price, the merchant will pay you a referral fee for initiating the sale.

Promoting affiliate products while paying fees on a monthly or yearly basis will allow you to create a steady stream of income without investing too much time and effort into it.

This factor largely depends on average customer retention so make sure you're choosing products that customers will be using for a while. For example, a product that will definitely be sticking around for around a year will be preferred over one that's likely to be popular for only a couple of months.

One misconception people have regarding affiliate marketing is that it's not legitimate. However, contrary to what some people may think, affiliate marketing is as credible as it gets. It is a completely legitimate way to monetize your blog. However, like every other online industry out there, there are scams everywhere. In order to avoid the traps, set by these scams, there are a few things you need to keep in mind.

First of all, legitimate affiliate marketing programs will never ask you to pay a fee. Additionally, the only way you can be paid through these programs is when you make a sale. In fact, this rule is also applied to two-tiered programs where some affiliate programs make money off of you when they make a sale and, hence, earn a commission.

Often times, you'll encounter affiliate programs that claim to be legit and promise to make you a lot of money by charging a "setup fee" or offer to give you a website a "website to market with" with a small amount of money in return. If you're facing a dilemma and aren't sure about whether or not you should trust these 'legitimate' affiliate programs, here's a hint: don't.

Considering that becoming an affiliate involves zero cost, you'd think there were no other ways to fall prey to a scam. Unfortunately, there are countless "informative" products and tools out there that vow to earn you a huge amount of income with little to no effort.
The best way to keep yourself safe from such scams is to ensure you're well-informed on the topic beforehand.

Furthermore, it is important for you to identify red flags, such as

Finding The Right Affiliate Programs

One of the best ways to find an affiliate program is by first checking whether the products and services you're interested in have an affiliate program, granted these products and services are something your followers would be interested in buying. Additionally, there are a number of others way you can turn to find products and services your audience is likely to be interested in.

The Best Of The Bunch

There are countless affiliate networks out there that can help you achieve your goals. In some circumstances, you might prefer turning to affiliate networks that are well-established and are linked to the most popular brands. These affiliate networks commonly include Commission Junction, Google Affiliate Network, Shareasale, Linkshare, and Pepperjam Network. *(Note: The links to these sites can be found at the Resources & Example Page)*

The obvious advantages to using these affiliate networks are that they have a history of being worth your money and will offer you management if you're still getting comfortable with the whole idea of affiliate marketing. On the other hand, however, these networks might not be able to provide you with customized attention and may not go out of their ways to help you. Furthermore, not all the in-house managers they've hired may be good. Apart from that, if you're still in the beginner stage and are still in the process of building a website for the programs you're aiming for, the task of getting approved for the programs in questions may prove to be more difficult than if you were working with a smaller affiliate network. Also, these networks take a longer time to pay you as compared to smaller networks which usually take around two weeks to do so. Lastly, these networks charge you more in terms of affiliate fees and commissions since they have the necessary resources for managing the payment of affiliates and connecting affiliates to advertisers.

e-Product Networks
These networks specialize in offering electronic products that can be downloaded instead of being shipped. Examples of such

products include eBooks and WordPress plugins, such as PLP Link Cloaker. Some of the most popular e-Product networks are Clickbank, Avangate, e-Junkie, and White Paper Source.

One of the biggest problems with this type of affiliate networks is that finding the right products to promote proves to be a real task. This is due to the fact that, most of the time the products in question aren't exactly legitimate. Obviously, this isn't the fault of the affiliate networks since they're not responsible for creating these products. Apart from that, it's really important for you to know which product is actually good without having to buy it yourself. Unless you're a household brand that automatically has access to free copies with the click of an email, you'll find this task to be heavy on the pocket.

Secondary Affiliate Programs

These affiliate programs are similar to the biggest affiliate networks, except that they work with small brands. Although these programs are reputable enough to ensure you're being paid, even in circumstances where merchants want to escape the scene, they may not be reliable in the long term and may not be around for a long time. However, they do pay more frequently than networks, such as Commission Junction and Shareasale. To be on the safe side, all you need to do is ensure reviews are favorable before you sign up.

What I personally believe is that you should always promote something that you already love. There is nothing better than endorsing something that you are familiar with since you can provide genuine insight into these products and services. And your genuine reviews are likely to sell these products and services faster.

In addition to this, one of the best ways to finding the right affiliate program yourself entails looking at what your competitors are doing. Figure out which products your competitors are promoting and look into the affiliate programs they're using. If you like what they're doing, there's no harm in taking a similar path.

TWO

PROS & CONS OF AFFILIATE MARKETING

By now you must be wondering whether affiliate marketing really is as viable an options as it seems. What are its highs and lows?

Like every other thing in this world, affiliate marketing obviously has its share of advantages and disadvantages. However, unlike many other things, there are ways to go about the cons of affiliate marketing. Due to this, let's take a look at the cons of affiliate marketing first!

Promoting Low-Quality Products May Negatively Affect Your Reputation

When you've established a loyal following that trusts you and will take your recommendations seriously, chances are your followers will purchase your recommended products and service despite the fact they may actually be rubbish. They will buy from you because, some way or another, you've succeeded in building a trustworthy relationship with them.

While establishing a good relationship with said followers, you also make them realize that they need a particular product or service in their lives or you successfully convince to buy the product you're endorsing.

However, there are many and I repeat, MANY, products out there that claim to do more than they actually can. Hence, it's important for you to maintain your quality and credibility and ensure that the products you're promoting offer real value, counter a need, and will maintain your followers' faith in you.

Low Product Commission Can Harm Your Affiliate Marketing Business

Many of us often make the mistake of working for far less than we deserve. In cases such as these, it is important to realize that with the same amount of effort, you could end up getting more than what you're currently earning.

Affiliate marketing works in the same way. Affiliate programs offer varying product commissions and some of them are not worth the time and effort you invest in promoting products.

Hence, it is important to know that getting leads and converting them into sales must generate a high enough commission to make affiliate marketing seem worthwhile as a whole.

Your time should never be free and you'll end up earning an extremely low return on investment (ROI) if you think it is.

Affiliate Marketing Can Become Isolating

When you venture off into the world of affiliate marketing on your own, trying to convince people to buy the products you're promoting, you may end up feeling lonelier than you would prefer.

So how do you overcome this loneliness while making sure you're doing something productive at the same time?

First of all, you need to properly define your target market and ensure you're networking within that market. By finding people who are interested in the same thing as you, not only will this give you an opportunity to learn, but it will even give you a sense of authority and help you expand your market. You can extend your networking by also groups on social media platforms, such as Facebook and LinkedIn and getting involved with other affiliate marketers.

Shutdown Of The Affiliate Company Or The Products

Similar to every other business out there, there's always a risk involved of it being closed off completely. To ensure you're reasonably protected against this unfortunate turn of events, you need to ensure you've performed extensive research into the product before you dive into its promotion. Moreover, to spread your risks, it is equally important to ensure you're not limiting yourself to just one product manufacturer or supplier.

By expanding you supply chain, you'll protect yourself against the loss you'll if one of them becomes bankrupt. Lastly, you also need to remember that although newer products on the market may seem exciting since they're more likely to provide a sudden flow of income, older products that have already secured their positions in the market and better if you're looking for a stable income stream in the long run.

Hijacked Affiliate Links

Although this con may appear pretty far-fetched, it's actually much more common than you think it is. Some competitors may become ruthless and may hijack your affiliate links. They do this by using software on your buyers' computers and replace your affiliate links with theirs. Hence, they're able to hijack your earnings without you even noticing it.

So, how do you prevent this from happening to you?

Well, there are two ways to go about this.

- You can use a website like TinyURL or bit.ly to cloak your affiliate links. This method is preferred if you're just a beginner, but there's a better way to protect yourself from hijacking.

- You can get a WordPress website and use a plugin like 'Pretty Links' or 'Redirection' on your website to cloak your links. This adds a few advantages of its own since your link will no longer look like an affiliate link and will actually look professional. Furthermore, you will also be able to track the clicks on your links more easily with the plugin.

Now that we've highlighted where you could go wrong with affiliate marketing, allow me to tell you about some of the countless benefits of affiliate marketing!

Close To Nothing Start-Up Costs

Let me tell you something you'll really like – you won't have to pay a single penny in order to promote a product. That's right, starting off in affiliate marketing costs nothing. You can simply jumpstart your new business by looking towards online training and community support and the various tools and resources available on the worldwide web.

Learn While You Work

It's true that, sometimes, experience helps you learn more than book learning ever would. Affiliate marketing is an area like this. When you're actively promoting your affiliate products and services, at the same time, you have the opportunity to do a multitude of things: learn, expand your business, and earn money from the sales you make in the process.

Creating A Global Market For Your Affiliate Products

One of the biggest advantages affiliate marketing has to offer is that its online nature allows your products to be exposed to anyone across the globe. The only thing you need to keep an eye out for is limiting your niche to an extent to prevent it from being too broad and focusing on the people who you think will actually be interested in your products.

Do What You Love By Choosing A Niche You Love

Affiliate marketing sets itself apart by ensuring that you don't need to follow a strict guide in succeeding. One of the pros this offers is that you can go for any niche you want to, be it sports, fashion, toys, kids, or even cooking. Of course, this niche needs to be realistic and shouldn't be something that cuts down your target audience.

Earn Passive Income with affiliate marketing

Affiliate marketing is one of the best ways to earn passive income. Promoting affiliate products while paying fees on a monthly or yearly basis will allow you to create a steady stream of income without investing too much time and efforts into it.

This factor largely depends on average customer retention so make sure you're choosing products that customers will be using for a while. For example, a product that will definitely be sticking around for around a year will be preferred over one that's likely to be popular for only a couple of months.

Avoid The Hassle Of Physically Handing The Products

With affiliate marketing, you'll always be the middle man. You don't need to go through the hassle of purchasing stock, forecasting sales, delivery the product, or even pay the heat/electricity expenses related to warehousing. All this falls under the responsibilities of the supplier.

THREE

CHOOSING THE BEST NICHE FOR YOURSELF

Once you've started to get the hang of affiliate marketing, you might ask yourself how you'll go about actually choosing a potential niche in affiliate marketing. In fact, not only do you need to choose a niche, but you need to determine how good it's going to be to help you achieve your goals.

I've said it before and I'll say it again – choose a niche you love and dive into it. Of course, by the sounds of it, this piece of advice may seem generic and something that every Tom, Dick, and Harry is going to tell you. However, you need to remember that there's a reason everyone's repeating the same advice over and over again.

Some might say anything that makes you money you'll eventually grow to love it. Obviously, earning income is a very good incentive to work. In the past, keeping this in mind, you could easily work on a niche like weight loss, the telecommunication industry, or the stock market. These topics might not be something you're passionate about, but they were still enough to get you by.

However, in this day and age, this won't work. Google is now verifying the identities of content authors, rewarding brands, and terminating any affiliate sites it thinks aren't contributing enough to the internet. The entire scope of affiliate marketing has changed.

Are there people who've figured out a way to trick Google? Do worthless affiliate websites still exist? These questions have the same answer: Yes. However, to ensure you're building a career in affiliate marketing and not just a means to get you by, for the time being, you need to pay heed to what I've just told you.

First, I'm going to tell you about a few ways you can brainstorm ideas for a potential niche. Next, I'll show you how you can evaluate your potential niches and how you can determine whether they're worth it or not.

How To Brainstorm Brilliant Ideas For Your Potential Niche

First of all, let me tell you that I won't be handing you a bunch of ideas on a silver platter. What I will do, however, is give you some advice on how you can find some brilliant market ideas.

What Are Your Hobbies?

Now, this one might seem as if I'm stating the obvious. However, you'd be surprised to know how many new affiliate marketers overlook this area. If you have something that you truly love doing and would prefer that over anything else in the world, it just might have the potential to become a profitable niche. Hence, it is important to realize that this hobby might just be the best way to start off.

However, at the same time, it's important to note not all hobbies are as profitable as they seem. In fact, some hobbies don't appear profitable at all and you might still be hell bent on squeezing some income out of it. For instance, I like coloring. I think it's an excellent way to relieve some stress, which is why I'm always on the lookout for the latest adult coloring books in every kind of bookshop there is. An added benefit of coloring books is that they're pretty easy on the pocket as well, so convincing your followers to spare $10 on the next big thing in the coloring book world might not be difficult at all.

The problem with this hobby – and countless other hobbies out there – is that it might not have the potential to be a profitable niche. Hence, in such circumstances, it's completely alright to not go for a niche based on your hobby if it doesn't have the potential to do something for you.

What Are You Friends' Hobbies?
Sometimes, the best ideas come from the people around you. Scroll through your Facebook newsfeed right now and see if you can figure out what people are usually interested in. Maybe

that guy from work is such an avid fan of football that he organizes his own tournaments? Did you know that?

There's so much you can learn by paying attention to people. You can even take it a step further by posting a status update on Facebook and asking the people on your friend's list about how they spend their spare time. When you're asking people, it's crucial for you to specify that you're looking for a niche that has the potential to be profitable. By doing this, whoever you ask will filter ideas according to what they perceive to be a profitable niche.

For example, let's say you have a friend who likes doing travel photography. They might look at what you're saying and think you might not be able to do it and, hence, not answer your question altogether. Due to this misconception, it's important to specify that you're actually trying to connect people who like doing something to the suppliers of their hobbies.

Research The Internet
When you have a resource like the internet available it to you, it's imperative for you to utilize it to its full advantage. Just

typing in simple terms, such as "pricey hobbies", "popular hobbies", or "profitable hobbies" will yield with hundreds of potential niche ideas if you're really determined to analyze the results. I'm sure you're bound to find something that you can imagine working out for you.

Pay attention to the supply side of the equation

You may not have thought of this before, but you can search for the term "supplies" on any keyword tool and learn a lot. There are many keyword tools out there, such as Google AdWords and SEMRush, will yield thousands of results. We often forget that people need supplies because they need them to do something else. Hence, these supplies are part of a niche. By going through these results, you'll be able to pick up something that might work for you. You can even sort the results by traffic volume or estimated CPC.

Accessories Everywhere

When you hear the word 'accessories', what comes to your mind? If you're like me, you'd probably think along the lines of shoes, jewelry, and phones. However, you'd be surprised to know how extensive your search on accessories would be. Not only your search include things you'd never even heard of before, but you'll also find out that these different types of accessories are pretty popular as well, in terms of web traffic.

Browse Through Magazines

There are millions of magazines being published every year and each one of these focuses on a niche. Hence, each one of these magazines has a potential audience out there through which you can make money.

You can explore your options on a website such as magazines.com and browse through the countless magazines you can subscribe to.

Although I highly recommend you to go for a niche that is truly profitable, you also need to remind yourself that you'll be publicly associated with it. Hence, whatever you choose needs to add value and fill a gap in your preferred niche. Choose a topic that, at the end of the day, YOU wouldn't mind being interested in either.

Now, once you have a bunch of ideas in your head, what criteria should you keep in mind in order to refine those ideas? Here's how.

Limit Your Niche While Still Leaving Room For Expansion
Let's say, you want to create a blog focusing on food recipes. The problem with this, however, is that this area is one of the most competitive areas out there and, hence, it will be extremely difficult for you to build an audience that's truly loyal to you. If your chosen niche seems to be broad and has too many competitors, perhaps you should consider narrowing it down. Where recipes are concerned, you can instead focus on recipes revolving around a particular diet or lifestyle, such as low-fat recipes, Paleo recipes, gluten-free recipes, dessert recipes, or even recipes including a particular ingredient like coconut oil. Every niche can be narrowed down to its sub-sects and you can take full advantage of these sub-sects. With that being said, before settling on a niche, it's important to understand how much potential it has in the long run as your brand grows.

Ensure An Audience Is There And That You'll Be Able To Reach Them

Once you've decided on a niche and think it's good enough, it is crucial for you to determine whether it's really worth it or not. One of the ways you can do that is by seeing whether your niche actually has a potential audience or not and whether you have the resources to reach that audience.

- Check how much your competition is spending on PPC advertising in your desired niche. If people aren't opting for paid advertising to promote themselves in your niche, then it may not be profitable.

- Check out your competition. Is your niche mainly dominated by a big brand or do indie blogs or subpages hold the latest share in the niche? Ensure the niche has room for you to be successful in.

- Check out how established your competition is. How much time and effort will you be required to invest in order to reach the top?

Ensure You're Willing To Do What It Takes

Continuing with the blog example, you'll notice that your biggest competitors will have high quality written all over them. Although this doesn't mean you need to be updated with everything your niche is doing, you still need to understand what it entails. For example, the majority of the successful bloggers go through the hassle of baking the recipes they post and take professional pictures of the food. Every niche you consider will have a specific minimum required if you want to succeed. Before signing up for more than you handle, you need to know whether you can truly meet the bare minimum of not. If you dive into a niche without the intention of truly competing, you're wasting your time and effort.

Verify That There Are Multiple Revenue Streams Within The Niche

You should never opt for a niche where your potential niche is going to be limited to a few merchants or avenues. You could possibly be stuck in a situation where you've built a website and have generated enough traffic to establish a following and just have a single affiliate program to finance it with. When that affiliate program shuts down, you won't have any way to move forward.

To prevent yourself from being stuck in a rut like this, make sure there are multiple affiliate programs available and there's advertiser demand as well. This will ensure that you have the opportunity to fall back on other revenue streams in case things don't work out with your primary affiliate program.

For instance, in a food blog, you can sell a variety of affiliate products such as appliances, utensils, and ingredients.

Check Out Whether Or Not The Niche Is Defensible

In today's day and age, it's important to go for a niche that offers your promotional opportunities outside traditional search engines. By opting for alternate methods, you'll be able to raise your rankings in the search engines. You can easily use social media platforms, such as Facebook, Pinterest, Google+ and Twitter, can be utilized to promote your blog and build your brand.

FOUR

AFFILIATE MARKETING THROUGH BLOGGING

Blogging, the act of posting your own content on an online journal or a blog, is a very popular platform these days. Nowadays, blogs are a means used by people as an online diary. The authors of blogs keep running accounts of their lives and, similar to a diary, a blog comprises entries or posts of the blog owner. Today, blogs are used by a wide array of professionals who use this platform to introduce the world to their art, music, videos, and photographs, and eventually sell them.

With the onset of the digital age, we now live in a world where information is accessible instantaneously with a few clicks on your phone. The majority of the world's population can gain access to information through the blessing that is the internet. Irrespective of which sector anyone belongs to, whether it is from financial service, real estate, education, or even fashion, blogging is a tool that can prove effective and efficient to anyone who decides to take the plunge.

There are a number of advantages a blog is able to provide and all of these contribute to helping you build your brand and your customer base. First of all, a blog allows your customers, existing and prospective, to find you easily. Every time you post something new on your blog, your blog will be ranked higher on Google or Yahoo, thanks to Search Engine Optimization (SEO).

Furthermore, when your customers can find you easily, it also gives them the chance to interact with you more. It provides them with a platform through which they can offer you feedback and suggestion, which enhances the trust they have in you. With a blog, you become more than a company; you become real.

And imagine how valuable this advantage would be if your competitors don't offer a blog of their own. When you create a blog, you share a part of yourself with your followers. Doing this is bound to give you a competitive advantage over your competitors when you establish and build an online presence for yourself, enabling you to stand out among hundreds of your competitors.

Now that you know a few of the many advantages blogging can offer you, you can refer to this *(link can be find on the resource page at the end)* guide to know how you can actually build your own blog. Now, I'll tell you how you can monetize your blog through affiliate marketing and take it a step further.

Build An Email Listing

Before you officially launch your blog, you should take out some time to build your email listing. Your blog won't earn you anything if you don't have a list of prospective customers and subscribers.

In order to build your email list, you can offer potential followers some incentives like a free eBook or training video. Also, make sure you're not just collecting email address, but you're collecting the names of their owners as well. Lastly, you can choose to use multiple methods to generate leads, such as generating a pop up through which readers may be directed to your blog.

Build A Relationship With Your Subscribers

Many bloggers make the mistake of stopping when they have enough subscribers on their email list. However, their work doesn't end there. You need to make sure your subscribers are loyal to you and your blog and this can only be done if you provide value by knowing who your subscribers and why they're choosing to read your blog. By answering the latter, you'll be able to solve their problems accordingly. Apart from that, you can even stay in touch with them by emailing them from time to time through email marketing software.

The last, and most important, thing you need to do is ensure you stand out in the crowd. You know how they say you can only be a small fish in a big pond or a big fish in a small pond? Well, I'm telling you can be a big fish in a big pond if you play your cards right. Set yourself apart by ensuring your blog has 'high-quality' written all over it. You can do this by making sure your content is interesting. Build a public presence by speaking at an event, giving interviews, getting professional pictures of yourself, and making videos of yourself speaking about the topic in question.

Through these tactics, you'll be able to present yourself as an expert in your field. The best bloggers out there don't just have a good grasp on blogging, but they have also successfully built an online business for themselves. You can do this too by always remembering that, by taking a shortcut, you'll never succeed. You need to invest time and effort into your blog and only then will you be able to reap your rewards. Additionally, if you're one of those people who learn more when they can visualize something, you might find it helpful to watch a video on YouTube that shows you how to build a blog, step by step.

FIVE

AFFILIATE MARKETING THROUGH PODCASTING

A lot of us may have an opinion regarding something, but do not have the ability to write it. Instead, we choose to talk. This is where podcasting comes in. Podcasters can easily broadcast anything of their choice with just a computer and a good internet connection.

Podcasts are proving to be quite popular as of late and many people, including celebrities and bloggers, are choosing to voice their opinions using this method. Many of us confuse podcasts with online streaming; the former can simply be downloaded and listened to whenever while the latter needs a constant internet connection. Nowadays, podcasts with videos, commonly known as vodcasts, are gaining popularity as well. Podcasts aren't just limited to individuals; businesses and groups can choose to create podcasts as well.

Setting up your own podcast, which you can learn through a [visual walkthrough](), can offer you a multitude of advantages. Some of these are:

- Making a podcast is much easier than making a video. All you need is your voice and a topic to focus on. A lot of people are camera shy, but that doesn't mean they can't express their opinions.

- When people listen to your podcast, they can relate to you more than they ever would through your words. They'll be able to know what you're feeling with your voice and, hence, feel what you feel. Your listeners will be able to connect to you on a completely different level.

- Sometimes, people get sick of writing. This doesn't mean that you start hating it; it just means you'd like to do something else for a change. As a blogger, I'm sure you must be looking for something else to do for a while being productive at the same time. Podcasts allow you to make your brain work in a similar manner while still doing something different.

Setting up your very own podcast might just open up a plethora of opportunities to you, including becoming a local celebrity. In order to reach that level, it is important to have a few strategies in mind to take your podcast to the next level.

- ❖ You need to first identify your target avatar. If you create your podcast and don't have anyone to talk to, you won't have anyone listening to you either.

- ❖ Additionally, you should give your podcast a particular theme. One you have your target audience in mind, you must go for your niche. If your podcast seems as if it doesn't have a specific theme going on, it's going to appear all over the place and no one's going to listen to it.

❖ Once you've begun to get a hang of creating podcasts and have established a stable following, you can start building upon them. Try your best and ensure you're offering the richest content possible and all the ideas you're promoting are in line with each other.

Now that your podcast has built its pace and you're generating quality content on a regular basis, sponsors will begin to take notice of you. The rate at which these sponsors decide to approach you will depend on the level of popularity you've succeeded in achieving.

These sponsors will begin negotiating with you and devise a deal. Sponsors usually offer a deal that is commonly known as the "Industry Standard". This Industry Standard has two parts:

❖ 15-second Pre-Roll: When you mention the product or service of your sponsor for fifteen seconds. It occurs before the podcast actually begins.

- 60-second Mid-Roll: When you mention the product or service of your sponsor for a minute, in the middle of the show. It usually occurs when the podcast is 40 – 70% complete.

Sometimes, you may even choose to mention your sponsors during your closing sequence when you're giving your closing remarks, or once they're done.

With all this being said, sometimes you may even choose to approach sponsors yourself. However, do keep in mind that the sponsors you have in mind can potentially benefit from your niche. This means that your sponsors need to be connected to your niche some way or another. When you're creating pre-rolls or mid-rolls, you'll be able to add these advertisements in a much smoother manner, without these sponsors appearing too out of place. Apart from that, you should also go for a sponsor you can trust. It will difficult to pitch something that you're not familiar with yourself. Due to the fact that your visitors can actually listen to you, unless you disguise it like an expert, they'll be able to tell when you're lying.

SIX

STRATEGIES TO MAKE THE MOST OF AFFILIATE MARKETING

When you hear the term 'affiliate marketing' oftentimes you may find yourself thinking that there's no easier way to make money. In fact, if you personally know a few affiliate marketers, they may even tell you it's the simplest thing they've ever done. However, let me be very honest with you; they're lying. Affiliate marketing is anything, but easy. Sorry to break it to you, but you aren't going to become a millionaire with affiliate marketing overnight. I'm not saying it's never going to happen, I'm just saying it requires the same amount of time and effort as anything else. The sooner you get used to this idea, the sooner you'll be able to put in your sweat and blood into this brilliant scheme. And when you do that, you'll be able to master this skill and make money while you sleep at night. So what's the best way you can earn the most out of affiliate marketing? Well, I'm going to tell you about a few strategies that'll make everything easier for you.

Trying To Achieve Too Much, Too Soon
Many beginners make the unforgivable mistake of trying to conquer as many niches as possible as soon as they start their careers in affiliate marketing.

You may hear countless stories about affiliate marketers making $50-$100 every day through Clickbank products by marketing products in every kind of emerging niche. However, most people make the mistake of owning tens of websites in the most random niches possible, without developing each of these, resulting in no sales.

Although it is definitely recommended for you to experiment with a number of niches, you should consider doing that once you've established yourself in one niche and you're satisfied with the leads your first website is generating.

Create Content That Your Competition Can't Compete With

One of the biggest struggles affiliate marketers commonly go through is proving their worth as middlemen in the value chain. Affiliates possess the secret advantage of making quick decisions and act on them with content marketing.

Whereas established brands spend up to months developing their content strategies and getting them approved by holding countless meetings, affiliates, on the other hand, have the opportunity to create high-quality content that competitors find difficult to compete with.

Qosy, a blog centered on travel, lifestyle, and homeware, publishes a 3,000 – 8,000-word guide every month or so. This guide focuses on difficult buying decisions and, although, not all of these posts include affiliate links, affiliate links are usually added when a site they recommend has an affiliate program.

Google tends to reject content that fails to add value and, by following a strategy like this, you'll be able to overcome this problem easily. The guides published by Qosy get shared up to 10,000 times and are used to educate their customers on their purchase decisions. Each requires about 40-50 hours of hard work and aims to beat the best possible content currently available.

Now, pay attention to what I just said. Providing high-quality content is crucial to the success of your blog. This content needs to seamlessly incorporate your affiliated links and, simultaneously, give your visitors the feeling that they're not wasting their time; the better your content, the greater the likelihood that it's going to show up on search engine you need to remember that your readers won't do anything you say unless they're getting something in return. This is exactly why the concept of previews is so popular; customers need to first know they're getting something valuable in return for buying the product or service you've recommended. For example, in the case of Qosy, their customers are getting the chance to learn how they can make better decisions. This way, customers get a glimpse of the quality you provide and know they're not giving something without, first, getting something in return.

If you're still confused about the way this works, take a look at one of the golden advice offered by [Gary Vaynerchuk](), one of the greatest names in marketing today. Gary Vaynerchuk came up with the concept of 'Jab, Jab, Jab, Right Hook'. Simply put, this concept highlights how you can create a following by giving your potential customer base as much as you possibly can, whether it's a preview, daily quotes, or even something as simple as a good morning. As long as your customers feel like they're getting something, they are more likely to give you something in return.

Build A Brand That Adds Value

Many affiliate marketers make the mistake of thinking of their platforms as just websites. This approach is all wrong since affiliate marketers rarely think of building a strong brand.

Today, Google is likely to favor affiliate marketing websites that appear to have strong brands. For example, if you conduct a little research on your own, the most successful affiliate marketing websites are websites in categories such as personal finance, travel, and homeware. All of these, like Moneysupermarket, Which, LastMinute.com, and Compare.com are strong brands that offer value to their customer and possess editorial integrity.

As time goes on, affiliate marketers will find themselves in a difficult position if they fail to establish a brand their customers can trust. Hence, it's important to keep this into consideration when you're building your website.

Keep The Mobile In Mind

In November 2014, mobile constituted 46 % of all affiliate links and 26 & of affiliate retail sales. Why is this important to you?

That's because if your website isn't mobile friendly, you're probably losing on a lot of potential commissions. Recently, Google also launched a mobile-friendliness checker and experimented with determining whether a website is mobile-friendly or not. Hence, building a website that's mobile-friendly is a good way to outrank your competitors with mobile-friendly platforms.

Additionally, this is also important because more and more people these days are purchasing goods and services from their smartphones. Due to this, some niches, products, and search criteria will quickly become popular and this can easily be capitalized by forward-thinking affiliates.

For information on how to build a mobile-friendly website, you can check out [Google Developers Mobile-Friendly](#) section.

Keep Track Of Breakout And Seasonal Trends
Affiliate marketers have been using trends as their secret weapon for a long time. Despite this, there are always new trends breaking out every day, giving way to new multi-million dollar niches every annually.

In order to find out what's popular and what's not, you need to first learn to differentiate between seasonal and breakout trends. The former are predictable, recurring, and allow you to prepare for them in advance.

Google Trends is a great way to know what's trending in which season. Not only can you just enter a keyword and find out how its search volume varies throughout the year you can even use the category function to find out which what's trending in specific seasons of particular industries.

Breakout trends are relatively harder to predict and even the most experienced of us find it difficult to predict the next six months of our industries. Despite this, a good way to start out is by going through the predictions of experts in your own industry. You can also find out which countries are likely to become popular in the near future and start promoting their hotels, flights, and any other products related to traveling there.

Lastly, there are also websites like TrendWatching that allow you to determine the direction the world is heading in. At the end of the day, though, the best way to know what's upcoming is by paying attention to your surroundings and draw interest towards your industry.

Aim For Topic Targeting Instead Of Keyword Targeting

Lately, Google has been trying to limit the SEO community's obsession with keyword targeting. It has now removed keyword data in Google Analytics, in addition to reducing exact-match targeting in Google Adwords. This makes it difficult for affiliate marketers to aim at individual keywords.

Although these changes may seem drastic at first, they're actually a blessing since it allows you focus more on topic-targeting and draw long tail traffic.

Rather than trying to rank your content at the top, you should aim to create in-depth posts about the topic in question.

Through this, you won't be over-focused on your ranking and will be more focused on attracting long-term traffic.

Conclusion

Money Making Mindset

"*Put your heart, mind, intellect and soul even to your smallest acts. This is the secret of success.*" – Swami Sivananda

Affiliate marketing is an amazing way you can monetize your blog and earn passive income online within 90 days. It's always a wise idea to earn money on the side in order to ensure you're financially secure in the future.

However, you don't just have to sign up for an affiliate program and promote whatever they're offering. What you promote should be in accordance with your beliefs as well and, at the end of the day, you should be happy with what you're doing. When you're getting involved with affiliate marketing, it might just end up taking all of your time so you need to play your cards right from the very beginning.

Be genuine and original. Don't just flood your website with countless products just because you can. I've repeated one thing over the course of this eBook and I'll say it again – quality. It doesn't matter if you're selling a couple of products, as long as the products and posts they're sandwiched in are high in quality, you're bound to succeed. Adopt the soft-sell approach to ensure you're engaging your readers for a long period of time.

When you take the right steps, you are definitely going to enjoy affiliate marketing. Like anything else that's worth it, it obviously requires its fair share of time and effort, but soon you'll know how beneficial all of it was.

RESOURCES & EXAMPLES

Affiliate Programs

http://www.cj.com

https://www.shareasale.com

http://www.linkshare.com/marketing

https://www.pepperjamnetwork.com

e-Product Networks

http://www.clickbank.com

http://www.avangate.com/

http://www.e-junkie.com/

http://www.whitepapersource.com

Link Cloaking Tools

https://prettylinkpro.com/tag/plp/

http://www.tinyurl.com

https://bitly.com/

https://wordpress.org/plugins/pretty-link/

SEO Programs

https://www.google.com.pk/adwords/

https://www.semrush.com

Social Media Platforms

http://www.pinterest.com

http://www.twitter.com

Blogging And Its Tools

https://wordpress.org

https://wordpress.org/plugin

Popular Bloggers to Learn From

http://www.johnchow.com/blog/

http://www.lukepeerfly.com/

http://zacjohnson.com/

https://sugarrae.com/all/

Podcasting

https://www.youtube.com/watch?v=_SmgdY7vfoo

Podcasts To Learn From

https://solopreneurhour.com/

https://mixergy.com/welcome/

http://www.smartpassiveincome.com/category/podcast/

Examples of Affiliate Marketing Websites

http://www.moneysupermarket.com/

http://www.which.co.uk

http://www.lastminute.com/

http://www.compare.com

Free eBook Club Invitation

Love Reading? Join Free eBook Club today to get "Mental Toughness Develop a Winner's Mindset and conquer success", totally free.

Click the link below to receive it:

https://greenprotein.leadpages.co/free-ebook-club/

In Mental Toughness, you will be introduced to a mindset that can assist you in tough times.

In addition to getting Mental Toughness, you will have the opportunity a variety of books for free.

Again here is the link to Join:

https://greenprotein.leadpages.co/free-ebook-club/

www.ingramcontent.com/pod-product-compliance
Lightning Source LLC
Chambersburg PA
CBHW071825200526
45169CB00018B/1020